to Barbara and Arthur Griffit'

Make a Joyful

T0087880

N (1988)

PSALM 100

© Copyright 1994 Novello & Company Ltd.

All Rights Reserved

Edward Gregson

Make a Joyful Noise

for SATB and Organ

ISBN 0-85360-338-3

9 780853 603382

NOVELLO

Order No. NOV 29 0677

Exclusive distribution: Centre,
Newmarket Road, Bur B

EXCLUSIVELY
DISTRIBUTED BY
HAL LEONARD
CORPORATION
14020417
U.S. $9.50

8 84088 42802 0

Composer's Note

My anthem *Make a Joyful Noise* has three main sections (fast-slow-fast) and is essentially jubilant in nature. After a brief introduction the choir enters, using as its text the first two verses of Psalm 100. This reaches a climax on the word 'singing' after which the music subsides into the serene key of C major for the female voices to sing a reflective tune on the words 'Know ye', surrounded by various counter-melodies. Male voices then take over this tune (inverted) and the final comment is left to unaccompanied choir, leaving sopranos on a held low D. At this point the last section begins. The style here takes off its hat to minimalism, with multi-layered textures underpinning the choral unisons on the word 'Enter'. Eventually the tonality heads towards G major and a reprise of the opening music, with a coda full of energetic exuberance.

Edward Gregson

Duration: 8 minutes

Make a Joyful Noise was commissioned by St. Dunstan's College, London, for its centenary celebrations in 1988. It was first performed by the combined choirs and instrumentalists of the College, conducted by Norman Harper, at the Fairfield Halls, Croydon, on 28 November 1988. This work has been recorded on Koch International Classics (3-7202-2H1) by the East London Chorus with the Locke Brass Consort and Paul Ayres (organ), conducted by Michael Kibblewhite.

The full version is scored for Choir, 4 Trumpets, 2 Horns, 3 Trombones, Tuba, Timpani, Percussion, and Organ. It is the composer's wish that whenever possible the full version is used in performance. However, this alternative version with organ accompaniment only may also be used. Full score and parts are available on hire from the publisher.

The composer gratefully acknowledges the assistance of Roger Wibberley in the preparation of this version.

©Copyright 1994 Novello & Company Ltd.
14 –15 Berners Street, London W1T 3LJ, UK
Exclusive distributor: Music Sales Limited,
Newmarket Road, Bury St Edmunds, Suffolk IP33 3YB, UK

4

* more voices on inner parts

un - to the Lord,_____

un - to the Lord,

un - to the Lord,_____

un - to the Lord,_____

145

- selves.

151

$\boxed{10}$

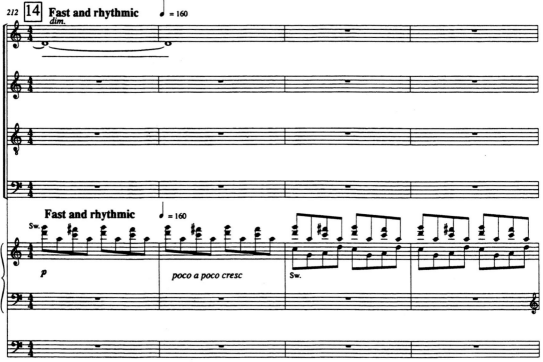

216

220

26

praise:_____ be thank - ful un - to him and

praise:_____ be thank - ful un - to him and

praise:_____ be thank - ful un - to him and

praise:_____ be thank - ful un - to him and

bless___ his name,_____ be thank - ful un - to him and

bless___ his name,_____ be thank - ful un - to him and

bless___ his name,_____ be thank - ful un - to him and

bless___ his name,_____ be thank - ful un - to him and

bless____ his name.____

bless____ his name.____

bless____ his name.____

bless____ his name.____

274

279 **19**

For the Lord___ is good,_____ for the

For the Lord___ is good,_____ for the

For the Lord___ is good,_____ for the

For the Lord___ is good,_____ for the